MW00880518

North Carolina DMV Written

Test Book (2024)

---A Quick Practice Test Guide----

DMV Permit/license Practice Test Questions and Answers for Car Drivers

James C. S. Bowen

Attribution

"Image: Freepik.com". The cover has been designed using assets from Freepik.com

Contents.

Preface

We offer all the materials you need to ace this exam! Purchase the practice test book right away to ensure that you are well-prepared for the **DMV** exam and that you pass it with flying colors!

By giving identical or extremely similar exam questions, the **"North Carolina DMV Test Book"** was specifically developed to guarantee the outstanding success of all driving test participants. We've made studying for the DMV test much easier by providing you with this concise practice and revision book. Our main goal is to prepare you for the exam and ensure that you do not have any difficulties during the exam.

The driving exam includes a variety of questions that will test your ability to think quickly and demand that you use common sense. The questions in this book will help you understand what to expect on the test and will boost your chances of getting your learner's permit or driver's license.

Your success is guaranteed if you use this manual as a rapid learning aid and a revision guide!

Practice test 1

49 Test questions:

1. **If you are guilty of tailgating, you will receive _____ points on your driving record.**

A) 3

B) 6

C) 5

D) 4

The correct answer is **D**

2. **If you are guilty of passing where signs or pavement markings forbid it, you will receive _____ points on your driving record.**

A) 4

B) 3

C) 5

D) 6

The correct answer is **D.**

3. **Which of the following may occur if you accumulate seven points?**

A) You might be asked to provide proof of financial responsibility.

B) Your driver's license may be suspended.

C) A driver improvement clinic may be required of you.

D) All of the aforementioned may occur.

The correct answer is C.

4. **If you are convicted of speeding in a school zone, you will receive ____ points on your driving record.**

A) 3

B) 5

C) 4

D) 2

The correct answer is A.

5. **Your second license suspension for having too many points will last**

A) 6 months.

B) 90 days.

C) One year.

D) 120 days.

The correct answer is A.

6. **What are your options in a two-way left-turn lane?**

A) Turn left to exit the road

B) Turn left to join the road

C) Overtake other vehicles

D) (a) or (b).

The correct answer is D.

7. **Your driver license will be cancelled for ____ years if you are convicted of DWI for the second time in three years.**

A) 4

B) 5

C) 2

D) 3

The correct answer is **A**.

8. **If you are convicted of drag racing on public roadways in North Carolina, your driver license will be suspended for**

A) four years.

B) a year.

C) Three years.

D) a period of two years.

The correct answer is **C**.

9. **A driver under the age of 18 who is guilty of a second moving infraction within a year may have his or her provisional license suspended for**

A) 15 days.

B) 90 days.

C) 30 days.

D) 60 days.

The correct answer is **C**.

10. This road sign means:

A) Lane closed for traffic.

B) There is a traffic signal ahead.

C) 4-way stop ahead.

D) Stop before turning right.

The correct answer is B

11. This road sign means:

A) No right turn.

B) No U-turns

C) All traffic turn right

D) Low clearance.

The correct answer is A

12. This road sign means:

A) No trucks allowed

B) Truck stop ahead

C) Trucks under 12,000 lbs. allowed

D) Hill or downgrade up ahead.

The correct answer is D

13. This road sign means:

A) One-way street ahead.

B) The right lane ends soon.

C) The left lane ends soon.

D) Highway entrance ramp ahead.

The correct answer is B.

14. This road sign means:

A) Pass with caution.

B) Railroad crossing.

C) Do not enter.

D) Yield the right-of-way.

The correct answer is C.

15. This sign warns drivers of:

A) a reduction of lanes.

B) a narrow road ahead.

C) a dip in the road. Drivers should be ready to stop if the dip is filled with water.

D) a bridge ahead, wide enough to accommodate two lanes of traffic, but with very little clearance.

The correct answer is D.

16. A 4-way stop sign means:

A) There are four stop signs at the intersection.

B) The first vehicle to reach the intersection should move forward first.

C) All traffic from all four directions must come to a standstill.

D) All of the above.

The correct answer is D.

17. This sign means:

A) road construction.

B) lane ends, merge left.

C) divided highway ahead.

D) narrow bridge ahead.

The correct answer is B.

18. When you see this sign, you:

A) need to brake suddenly.

B) should be prepared to make sharp turns at a high speed.

C) should not speed up or brake quickly.

D) need to be prepared to immediately turn right and then left..

The correct answer is C.

19. This road sign means:

A) Winding road ahead.

B) Slippery when wet.

C) No U-Turn.

D) Sharp curve ahead.

The correct answer is B.

20. This sign warns that:

A) the bridge ahead is wide enough for only one vehicle at a time.

B) the pavement ends.

C) traffic must merge left.

D) traffic must merge right.

The correct answer is C.

21. The minimum drinking age in North Carolina is _____ years.

A) 18

B) 9

C) 21

D) 20

The correct answer is C.

22. When you see a green arrow and a red traffic signal,

A) it implies that all cars traveling in the direction of the arrow must come to a complete stop.

B) don't follow the arrow until the signal turns green.

C) travel with caution in the direction of the arrow

D) the road ahead is closed to traffic; take the arrow.

The correct answer is C.

23. What should you do if a train passes?

A) Watch for a green light.

B) Drive your car across the train tracks.

C) Blow the horn and continue driving.

D) Check for incoming trains once more and proceed with caution.

The correct answer is D.

24. Other than alcohol, what drugs can impair your driving ability?

A) Antihistamines.

B) Marijuana.

C) A cold therapy.

D) All of the above.

The correct answer is D.

25. When passing a bicyclist, do the following moves:

A) To warn the bicyclist, sound the horn.

B) Move as far to the left as you possibly can.

C) Maintain your position in the center of the travel lane.

D) Switch on your four-way flashers.

The correct answer is B.

26. Vehicle seat belts are particularly effective as an injury prevention device when used by:

A) The driver.

B) Passengers on a long journey.

C) All passengers in a car traveling on an expressway.

D) Any and all occupants of a vehicle at any time.

The correct answer is D.

27. To avoid accidents, drivers should communicate with one another by:

A) Signaling when changing lanes, slowing down, or halting.

B) The use of their horns in crises and whenever it is essential.

C) The use of their emergency flashers or signals as needed.

D) All of the above.

The correct answer is D.

28. Use _____ to indicate that you are turning if your turn signals fail.

A) horn

B) headlights

C) hand signal

D) warning lights

The correct answer is C

29. If a driver consumes alcohol before driving, they should remember that alcohol has the largest impact on their _____.

A) hearing

B) vigilance

C) point of view

D) decision

The correct answer is D.

30. When parking near the curb on an incline, point the front wheels as follows:

A) Into the muck.

B) Away from the curb.

C) Towards or away from the curb.

D) Forward.

The correct answer is B.

31. You will be turning left from a left-turn lane when a yellow arrow appears in your lane. To cross the junction, you should:

A) Accelerate.

B) Stop instantly and never turn around.

C) Prepare to respond to the incoming signal.

D) Cross the intersection since you have the right-of-way.

The correct answer is C.

32. When _____, you have the right of way.

A) you enter a traffic circle

B) you are backing out of a driveway

C) you're leaving a parking garage

D) you are already in a traffic circle

The correct answer is D.

33. When a school bus comes to a stop with its red lights flashing, what does it mean?

A) You may proceed if there are no children on the road.

B) You should not pass.

C) You may proceed if you are facing the front of the bus.

D) If it is on the opposite side of a dual road, you may not be able to pass.

The correct answer is B.

34. A rectangular road sign implies the following:

A) A crossing guard at a school.

B) A railroad crossing.

C) Stop.

D) The posted speed limit.

The correct answer is D.

35. When is it permissible to drive in a carpool lane?

A) When you have attained the specified minimum number of passengers.

B) When operating a 15-passenger van without passengers.

C) When you need to pass the vehicle in front of you.

D) When you are in a hurry.

The correct answer is A.

36. What should you do if you come across this sign?

A) Stop completely, look for pedestrians, and drive across if the road is clear.

B) Reduce your speed without completely stopping.

C) Stop entirely and wait for a green light.

D) Reduce your speed and keep an eye out for traffic.

The correct answer is A.

37. What is the correct traffic signal sequence from top to bottom:

A) Red, yellow, and green.

B) Red, green, and yellow.

C) Green, red, and yellow.

D) Green, yellow, and red.

The correct answer is A.

38. A broken white center line on the road, as shown in the illustration, indicates:

A) There are no approved turns.

B) Proceed with caution.

C) You are now in a no-passing zone.

D) You should proceed with caution when changing lanes.

The correct answer is D.

39. The following is one of the defensive driving guidelines:

A) Keep your gaze straight ahead as you drive.

B) Maintain vigilance and roaming vision.

C) Expect other drivers to compensate for your mistakes.

D) Ensure you can avert danger at the last possible moment.

The correct answer is B.

40. This traffic sign says:

A) Continue to the right.

B) On the right, yield.

C) Slower vehicles should proceed in the right lane.

D) At the next intersection, you must turn right.

The correct answer is A.

41. Keep an eye out for motorcyclists before changing lanes because

A) it is against the law for motorcycles to share traffic lanes.

B) of their small size, they are more difficult to see by others.

C) they have priority at intersections.

D) they have the right of way on the highway.

The correct answer is B.

42. This traffic sign warns you of the following:

A) A fork in the road.

B) A crossing for pedestrians.

C) There is a railroad crossing.

D) An exploding zone.

The correct answer is C.

43. A police officer directs you to proceed even if the traffic light is red. What should you do?

A) Hold your breath and wait for the green light.

B) Alter your lane and drive slowly.

C) Follow the officer's directions.

D) Come to a complete halt and wait for the officer to approach.

The correct answer is C.

44. Two sets of solid double yellow lines at least two feet apart:

A) Indicates an entry to a private driveway.

B) Should be regarded as a solid impassable barrier.

C) Indicates a lane for beginning or ending left-hand turns.

D) Denotes a center turn lane.

The correct answer is B.

45. Getting ready to smoke and driving while smoking

A) have no bearing on driving.

B) assist in keeping concentration.

C) are distracting activities.

D) are annoying driving habits.

The correct answer is C.

46. A car has come to a halt at a red light. Despite the fact that the light turns green, other vehicles remain in the junction. The driver should:

A) Wait for the vehicles to clear the intersection before proceeding.

B) Continue as long as they can safely maneuver around the other vehicles.

C) Wait for traffic to clear before entering the intersection.

D) Proceed to the junction after honking their horn to alert other drivers of their presence.

The correct answer is A.

47. You are driving in a large truck's blind spot if you

A) maintain a close proximity to its left front wheel.

B) are unable to see the driver in its side mirrors.

C) maintain a distance of at least 10 feet behind the large vehicle.

D) None of the preceding.

The correct answer is B.

48. **Your blind spot is the area of the road where**

_____

A) is just behind your vehicle.

B) you can see in your rearview mirror.

C) you can see in your side mirrors.

D) to see, you must turn your head.

The correct answer is D.

49. **If the ramp where you depart a highway slopes downward, you should:**

A) Adhere to the posted freeway speed limit.

B) Drive around the bend without braking.

C) Reduce speed to a safe level before the curve.

D) Accelerate to avoid oversteering before the turn.

The correct answer is C.

Practice test 2

40 Test questions:

1. **If you have to cross railroad tracks before an intersection during rush hour, you should:**

A) stop between the gates in case they close.

B) come to a complete stop on the tracks while waiting for the light to turn green.

C) hold off until you can fully traverse the tracks.

D) make a lot of horn blasts.

   The correct answer is C.

2. **When approaching a blind pedestrian who is using a white cane or utilizing a guide dog, you should:**

A) slow down and prepare to stop.

B) have the right of way, so continue.

C) continue as usual.

D) travel as far as you can by vehicle.

   The correct answer is A.

3. **Directions given by traffic officers _____ signs, signals or pavement markings.**

A) must obey

B) take precedence over

C) are less important than

D) never take precedence over

The correct answer is B.

4. In case of skidding, drivers should NEVER:

A) steer the car into the direction of the skid.

B) pump the brakes gently if they are about to hit something.

C) tap the gas pedal with their foot.

D) take their foot off the gas pedal.

The correct answer is C.

5. When getting ready to change lanes, you should:

A) quickly turn your head to check for other vehicles.

B) check your side view mirror.

C) check your rearview mirror.

D) All of the above.

The correct answer is D.

6. Your red traffic signal changes to green while a pedestrian is crossing in your traffic lane. The right of way should be given:

A) by the pedestrian, but only when vehicles are turning left.

B) by the pedestrian.

C) to you.

D) to the pedestrian.

The correct answer is D.

7. Which of the following must you obey over the others?

A) Flashing red light.

B) Red light.

C) Stop sign.

D) Police officer.

The correct answer is D.

8. A vehicle is stopped at a crosswalk to allow a pedestrian to cross the roadway. The driver of the vehicle approaching from the rear should:

A) overtake and pass the stopped vehicle.

B) not overtake and pass the stopped vehicle.

C) sound the horn.

D) None of the above.

The correct answer is B.

9. Air bags are meant to _____ seat belts.

A) protect

B) replace

C) fix

D) work with

The correct answer is D.

10. **When travelling at night with no other vehicles in front, you should use:**

A) high beam lights.

B) emergency flashers.

C) parking lights.

D) low-beam lights.

The correct answer is A.

11. **Drivers should be aware that a motorcyclist may:**

A) move to the center of the lane on steel deck bridges.

B) decrease speed and rise off the seat when approaching a railroad crossing.

C) quickly change speed or lane position.

D) All of the above.

The correct answer is D.

12. **These symptoms are linked with drowsy driving:**

A) You continue to yawn.

B) You forgot driving the last few miles.

C) Your eyes go out of focus.

D) All of the above.

The correct answer is D.

13. **What is the meaning of a flashing red light?**

A) The light will soon change to constant red.

B) Drive with care.

C) Proceed, but yield to other traffic at the intersection.

D) The same as a STOP sign.

The correct answer is D.

14. What does a yellow arrow mean?

A) The same as a steady yellow light.

B) If you intend to turn in the direction of the arrow, be prepared to stop.

C) Do not go in the direction of the arrow.

D) None of the above.

The correct answer is B.

15. A car driver wishes to turn right at the intersection. A pedestrian with a guide dog is about to cross the street in front of the car at the corner. They driver should do the following before turning right:

A) Stop driving until the pedestrian crosses the street.

B) When it is safe to cross, notify the pedestrian.

C) Wait until the pedestrian crosses the street.

D) To warn pedestrian of their presence, sound the horn.

The correct answer is C.

16. When entering traffic from a stop, you should:

A) travel 200 feet slower than the rest of the traffic.

B) allow adequate space to catch up to traffic speed.

C) before entering the lane, wait for the first vehicle to pass.

D) expect people to make way for you to enter.

The correct answer is B.

17. This does this symbol represent?

A) Enter the road ahead only if it is safe to do so.

B) The road in front of you is closed in both directions.

C) You are not permitted to make a U-turn when you see this sign.

D) The route ahead of you has been closed in your direction.

The correct answer is D.

18. What should you do if your phone rings while you're driving and you're a minor?

A) Answer the phone if you have a hands-free device.

B) Please leave a message on voice mail.

C) If it is from your parents, take the call.

D) Inform the caller that you will return their call later.

The correct answer is B.

19. When a driver is double-parked in a traffic lane:

A) they should always utilize their emergency flashers.

B) they've become stranded on the side of the road due to strong fog.

C) their car has broken down on the side of the road.

D) they are fatigued after late-night driving.

The correct answer is C

20. What does a traffic signal with a red arrow pointing to the right, as seen below, means?

A) Go right after coming to a complete stop.

B) Before going right, wait for the light to turn green.

C) Go right after slowing down and watching for traffic.

D) Go right if there are no cars on the road at the time.

The correct answer is B.

21. What effect does alcohol have on your driving ability and judgment?

A) It enhances driving abilities while diminishing judgment.

B) It hinders driving skills as well as judgment.

C) It has no impact on driving skills or judgment.

D) It has no effect on judgment, however it does affect driving abilities.

The correct answer is B.

22. _____, if an approaching vehicle fails to dim its high-beam headlights at night.

A) Look toward the center of the road

B) Look towards the right side of your lane

C) Examine the left side of your lane

D) Keep a straight line in your lane

The correct answer is B.

23. **What does an orange and red sign with this shape means?**

A) Oncoming traffic must be given the right-of-way.

B) The car has priority.

C) A vehicle that moves slowly.

D) An emergency vehicle is on its way.

The correct answer is C.

24. **Tailgating another vehicle:**

A) assist drivers in avoiding the blind spots of others.

B) is a frequent cause of rear-end collisions.

C) enhances fuel efficiency.

D) is an important part of the normal driving practice.

The correct answer is B.

25. **Before alternating lanes on a multi-lane highway, a driver should:**

A) flip on the headlights

B) sound the horn

C) inspect their mirrors for possible blind spots

D) reduce their speed of travel

The correct answer is C.

26. **Keep the following in mind when passing in the approach lane on a two-lane road, as shown in the example:**

A) Your comparative speed, as well as your ability to accelerate.

B) The quantity of clear space you wish to traverse.

C) Oncoming traffic speed and separation, as well as potential hazards.

D) All of the above options are correct.

The correct answer is D.

27. **When approaching a tight bend in the road, such as the one depicted, you should do the following:**

A) Apply the brakes as soon as you enter the curve.

B) Before entering the curve, use the brakes.

C) Drive into the bend, and then brake out of it.

D) Increase your speed as you approach the curve to gain more traction.

The correct answer is B.

28. **Teenagers who drive are more likely to be involved in an accident if they are:**

A) driving as a passenger with a peer.

B) driving in the company of adult passengers.

C) having adolescent passengers in the car.

D) traveling alone.

The correct answer is C.

29. **Which of the following statements concerning diamond-shaped signs on autos is CORRECT?**

A) They are not permitted to go on highways.

B) They are not allowed to exceed 35 miles per hour.

C) They must come to a complete stop before crossing the train tracks.

D) They always have priority over others.

The correct answer is C.

30. **When parking, turn your front wheels toward the curb:**

A) on an elevation.

B) on a level road.

C) looking downward.

D) close to a fire hydrant.

The correct answer is C.

31. _____if the road has a solid yellow line on one side and a broken yellow line on the other.

A) Pass only in an emergency

B) Pass if you're on an expressway

C) If the traffic is clear, proceed

D) Only cross at an intersection

The correct answer is C.

32. A red and white triangle at a crosswalk indicates:

A) an emergency vehicle is on the approach.

B) you should look all ways before crossing the street.

C) at the crossroads, come to a complete stop.

D) reduce your speed and make sure you have the ability to stop if required.

The correct answer is D.

33. Before merging into a motorway, you should _____ to check traffic.

A) use mirrors on both the inside and outside

B) make use of the rearview mirrors

C) glance in all mirrors and twist your head

D) look in your car's left-side mirror

The correct answer is C.

34. **What are the colors of the warning indicators that warn of potential dangers/hazard?**

A) White background with black text.

B) Yellow background with black text.

C) Text or symbols in blue with white letters.

D) Green background with white text.

The correct answer is B.

35. **Who is responsible for understanding how medications influence your ability to drive?**

A) You.

B) Your doctor.

C) The chemist.

D) The employee of the DMV.

The correct answer is A.

36. **A diamond-shaped sign is referred to as _____ symbol.**

A) interstate highway

B) school crossing

C) speed limit

D) risk on the road

The correct answer is A.

37. **When parking downhill without a curb, your car's front wheels must be directed:**

A) approaching the road.

B) parallel to the road.

C) in the direction of the roadside.

D) in the traffic direction.

The correct answer is C

38. **When driving in sluggish traffic and need to cross railroad tracks, you should:**

A) use your horn as you cross the tracks.

B) come to a complete stop on the tracks while waiting for the light to turn green.

C) if the gates close, come to a halt between them.

D) proceed once you have completely crossed the tracks.

The correct answer is D.

39. **Failure to inflate your car's tires to the manufacturer's requirements may result in:**

A) Poor gas mileage.

B) Inconsistent tire wear.

C) Ineffective steering.

D) All of the above.

The correct answer is D.

40. What does this symbol entail?

A) Come to a halt.

B) You're getting close to a school; keep a look out for children.

C) A shopping area ahead.

D) Pedestrians should walk on the sidewalk.

The correct answer is B.

Practice test 3

40 Test questions

1. **Why should you never depend on your mirrors when you prepare to change lanes?**

A) Mirrors are useless.

B) Mirrors leave "blind spots" behind both sides of vehicles.

C) Mirrors need to be adjusted.

D) You should look over your shoulder instead.

The correct answer is B.

2. **Aggressive driving involves:**

A) yelling, honking, gesturing at other drivers.

B) quick lane changes without a signal.

C) chasing or challenging other drivers.

D) All of the above.

The correct answer is D.

3. **On what three conditions does your blood alcohol content (BAC) hinge?**

A) Your weight. The quantity of alcohol you consume. How much time passes between drinks.

B) Your fitness state. How much alcohol you drink. Your height.

C) Your weight. The type of beverage you drink. How fit you are.

D) Your height. How much alcohol you drink. The type of beverage you drink.

The correct answer is C.

4. If your brakes are wet, you can dry them by:

A) Pulling over to the right and wait until it stops raining.

B) Increasing your speed while obeying the speed limit.

C) Lightly pressing the gas and brake pedals at once.

D) None of the above.

The correct answer is C.

5. On average, how long does it take your body to remove the alcohol in 5 ounces of wine?

A) 3 hours.

B) 30 minutes.

C) one hour.

D) 10 minutes.

The correct answer is C.

6. When driving on slippery roads, drivers should:

A) change lanes quickly.

B) avoid crossing bridges or intersections.

C) brake harder than usual.

D) increase their following distance.

The correct answer is D.

7. **What is a probable reaction when you take another drug while you drink alcohol?**

A) The effects of the alcohol and the drug are enhanced.

B) There are no effects, unless the drug is prescription only.

C) If the drug is over-the-counter, there are no effects.

D) The effects of alcohol are reduced by the drug.

The correct answer is A.

8. **At a stop sign there is no stop line or crosswalk. You must stop:**

A) after you enter the intersection, if you have a clear view of traffic on the intersecting roadway.

B) only if the traffic signal turns red.

C) at the next crosswalk.

D) before you enter the intersection.

E) **The correct answer is D.**

9. **If another vehicle is in danger of colliding with you, you should:**

A) flash your brake lights.

B) sound your horn.

C) use your emergency lights.

D) flash your headlights.

The correct answer is B.

10. The traffic light is green and you want to drive straight through an intersection. If a car is already in the intersection and is making a turn, you must:

A) move into the intersection and then stop.

B) wait for the next green light to appear.

C) allow the car complete its turn before you enter the intersection.

D) proceed through the intersection. You have precedence over others.

The correct answer is C.

11. In heavy rain, tires can begin to ride on the water that is covering the road pavement. This is called:

A) pavement-planing.

B) waterplaning.

C) hydroplaning.

D) rideplaning.

The correct answer is C.

12. The road has the most slippery surface:

A) During a heavy rainstorm or thunderstorm.

B) Immediately after the rain.

C) As soon as it starts raining.

D) In the midst of a light rain.

The correct answer is C.

13. One broken line signifies:

A) you can pass other vehicles and change lanes, if it is safe.

B) you cannot pass other vehicles or go across the line.

C) you can change lanes, but only when traffic conditions or obstructions in the road make it necessary.

D) None of the above.

The correct answer is A.

14. If your brakes fail while driving, do the following:

A) Change gears and look for a safe area to slow down and halt.

B) Press the brake pedal quickly; if this has no effect, release the parking brake.

C) If possible, pull over to the side of the road and call for help.

D) All of the above are correct.

The correct answer is D.

15. A driver is waiting at a red light to turn right, and a pedestrian on the driver's right side is waiting to cross the street in which the driver desires to enter. When the light turns green, who takes precedence?

A) The pedestrian.

B) The car has the right-of-way if the crossing is unmarked.

C) The driver because their signal is green.

D) The motorist has the right of way if they move first.

The correct answer is A.

16. **What should you do if you hear a siren or see a flashing red light from an approaching emergency vehicle but you are not yet at the intersection?**

A) Proceed slowly in the right lane until it has past.

B) Quicken your pace to stay ahead of it.

C) Come to a complete stop and pull over to the right side of the road.

D) Any of the above options.

The correct answer is C.

17. **In which of these situations should you follow the "three-second rule"?**

A) The area around your vehicle's flanks.

B) The space directly in front of your vehicle.

C) The space in your car's trunk.

D) The immediate vicinity of your automobile.

The correct answer is B.

18. **If you eat and drive, you will:**

A) make no mistakes on the road.

B) find it difficult to drive slowly.

C) be a better driver because you are not hungry.

D) be having difficulty driving.

The correct answer is D.

19. **If you need to slow down or come to a complete stop when other drivers are not expecting it, you should do the following:**

A) Use your emergency brake.

B) Look behind you for vehicles that may be in your blind area.

C) Gently press the brake pedal.

D) Prepare to honk your horn.

The correct answer is C.

20. **What happens if a person is in the middle of a block at a crosswalk, as shown?**

A) He has the right-of-way.

B) He must give up the right-of-way.

C) Vehicles have the right of way, but drivers must keep pedestrians in mind.

D) When approaching a crossing, automobiles must sound the horn to alert pedestrians that they must cross swiftly.

The correct answer is A.

21. What does this road sign indicate?

A) Continue to the next intersection.

B) A divided roadway nears its finish.

C) There is a one-way street ahead.

D) The road ahead has been closed.

The correct answer is B.

22. What should you do if the vehicle in front of you begins to pass you?

A) Keep your speed consistent so that traffic moves smoothly.

B) Slow down and come to a complete stop to allow the vehicle to pass.

C) Maintain a little speed reduction and keep to your lane.

D) Let the car pass by honking your horn.

The correct answer is C.

23. On a freeway, if you notice orange construction cones and signage, you must:

A) change lanes and maintain your current speed, or slow down.

B) plan ahead of time to avoid running into construction employees and equipment.

C) slow down since the lane is closing.

D) quicken your pace to avoid rubbernecking.

The correct answer is B.

24. Worn or bald tires, such as the one shown:

A) Reduce overall control while increasing stopping distance.

B) Create hydroplaning.

C) Cause tire failure and/or blowouts.

D) None of the preceding.

The correct answer is C.

25. If you observe red emergency lights or hear the sirens of an oncoming emergency vehicle, you must either:

A) move quickly to clear traffic.

B) move slowly till it passes.

C) stop at the right edge of the road.

D) stop completely at the intersection.

The correct answer is C

26. When driving by the children's play area, keep the following in mind:

A) Recognize when it is safe to cross the street.

B) Before crossing, come to a complete stop at the curb.

C) To arrive unexpectedly in front of you.

D) Only cross if accompanied by an adult.

The correct answer is C.

27. A driver may travel on the left half of a two-way roadway if:

A) there is a double yellow center line.

B) there is a solid line on their side of the center line.

C) passing is both safe and permissible.

D) the driver is nearing a corner and intends to turn left.

The correct answer is C.

28. **When can you drive around or under a railroad crossing gate?**

A) At no time.

B) When you have vision in both directions.

C) When the gate does not appear to be properly operating.

D) When you believe you will be able to drive through before it rains.

The correct answer is A.

29. **If a traffic signal light fails, you must:**

A) stop completely if other cars are present.

B) reduce your speed and, if necessary, come to a complete stop.

C) stop, and then continue when it is safe.

D) proceed normally through the junction.

The correct answer is C.

30. **What colors do traffic signs use to indicate the distance to the next highway exit?**

A) Yellow with black writing on a yellow background.

B) White letters on a black backdrop.

C) White letters on a yellow background.

D) White letters on a green background.

The correct answer is D.

31. You may be permitted to drive over a sidewalk to:

A) avoid driving over a speed bump.

B) drive into or out of a driveway or alley.

C) make a U-turn.

D) avoid being stuck in traffic.

The correct answer is B.

32. When driving on icy roads, you should

A) reduce the distance you look ahead of your vehicle.

B) come to a complete stop and test your tires' traction when ascending slopes.

C) avoid sharp turns and abrupt stops.

D) at all costs, avoid driving.

The correct answer is C.

33. If you see a green arrow pointing to the left, you can perform the following actions:

A) You can go in any direction.

B) Make a careful left turn.

C) Turn left or keep going straight.

D) If there are no vehicles approaching from the opposite direction, turn left.

The correct answer is B.

34. What does this symbol represent?

A) Stop if there is oncoming traffic.

B) There is a three-way intersection.

C) Crossroad.

D) Railroad crossing

The correct answer is D.

35. What does this symbol represent?

A) There is a two-lane road ahead; keep an eye out for oncoming traffic.

B) The road ahead is narrowing; prepare to merge to the right.

C) Traffic in the lane you're travelling in merges ahead.

D) A split highway ahead.

The correct answer is C.

36. You may drive in a carpool lane if you:

A) have the fewest number of passengers as specified on the sign.

B) are driving an empty 15-passenger van.

C) wish to pass the vehicle in front

D) are in a rush.

The correct answer is A.

37. Your left arm and hand are stretched downward, as shown in the image. This hand signal expresses your intention to _____.

A) turn left

B) turn right

C) stop

D) continue

The correct answer is C.

38. If you are driving and feel weary and drowsy, you should do one of the following:

A) get some fresh air and drink some coffee.

B) play loud music while speaking with other passengers.

C) stop and take a break.

D) Any of the prior options.

The correct answer is C.

39. Interpret the following road sign:

A) Only pedestrians may cross.

B) There is a traffic light ahead.

C) There are some trekking trails ahead.

D) There is a school crossing ahead.

The correct answer is D.

40. What does this symbol represent?

A) Children having a good time.

B) Bicycle rentals are offered.

C) Proceed to the parking entrance, keeping an eye out for oncoming traffic.

D) A bikeway crosses the road; keep an eye out for cyclists.

The correct answer is D.

Road signs test

69 Test questions

1. **The following shape is used:**

A) specifically for stop signs.

B) to notify drivers of present or potential hazards on the road.

C) for yield signals.

D) stop signs and railroad advance warning signs are examples of these.

   The correct answer is A

2. **What does a yellow arrow indicate?**

A) The same as the yellow light, but only applies to movement in the arrow's direction.

B) Vehicles traveling in all directions must come to a complete stop if possible. The light will turn red soon.

C) The equivalent of a green light.

D) None of the preceding.

The correct answer is A.

3. **This symbol denotes:**

A) The speed limit at night is 45 mph.

B) The suggested speed limit is 45 miles per hour.

C) The lowest speed restriction is 45 miles per hour.

D) If you're driving at night, take Route 45.

The correct answer is A.

4. **This symbol denotes:**

A) A U-turn is imminent.

B) A hairpin turn awaits.

C) Right turns are not permitted.

D) A sharp right turn awaits.

The correct answer is B.

5. This sign indicates:

A) Vehicles are only permitted to turn left.

B) For left turns, the middle lane is shared.

C) Left turns are not authorized in either direction of travel.

D) All of the above.

The correct answer is B

6. This road sign indicates:

A) Merge.

B) Change of lane.

C) Hospital parking ahead.

D) Crossroads.

The correct answer is D.

7. This sign cautions motorists that:

A) a double curve awaits them ahead.

B) they must either turn right or left.

C) the path ahead is twisty.

D) there is a junction ahead.

The correct answer is C.

8. This road sign indicates:

A) Wrong Way.

B) Merging Traffic.

C) Curve.

D) Road Work Ahead.

The correct answer is C.

9. This regulation sign informs drivers that:

A) at the next intersection, cars in the left lane must turn left.

B) traffic in the right lane must proceed straight.

C) all vehicles must immediately turn left.

D) None of the preceding

The correct answer is A.

10. The following is the meaning of this road sign:

A) A four-way stop is approaching.

B) The road ends ahead.

C) "Y" intersection.

D) A road branches off to the right.

The correct answer is C.

11. What does the following sign imply?

A) Reduce your speed to allow for an emergency vehicle.

B) When crossing the street, look both ways.

C) At the intersection, always come to a complete halt.

D) Keep moving more slowly and be ready to halt if required.

The correct answer is D.

12. What should a driver be most concerned about when they encounter this sign?

A) Driving with misaligned headlights; one side of the car is higher than the other.

B) Avoid damaging a tire if it drifts onto the shoulder.

C) Hydroplaning if the shoulder is wet.

D) Loss of vehicle control if the vehicle slides onto the shoulder due to a drop off.

The correct answer is D.

13. This symbol signifies:

A) If you see a car approaching, slow down and prepare to stop.

B) Stop, then continue when it is safe to do so.

C) Proceed gently across the junction without stopping.

D) Only halt completely when you reach an intersection.

The correct answer is B.

14. When you observe the following black-and-yellow traffic sign, what does it mean?

A) The road to the right has only one way traffic.

B) Due to road construction, take a right turn.

C) Slow down since the road ahead unexpectedly changes course.

D) Up ahead, cross the road to the right.

The correct answer is C.

15. What does this symbol below imply?

A) A sharp right curve.

B) A double curve stretches first to the right, then to the left.

C) There is a double curve from left to right.

D) The road comes to a halt in front of you.

The correct answer is B.

16. What does this symbol mean?

A) All vehicles must turn right.

B) The next detour.

C) All traffic must go in a straight line.

D) Do not take a right.

The correct answer is B.

17. **What maneuvers can be performed when driving in the center lane?**

A) Left turns.

B) U-turns.

C) Slower-moving cars overtaking.

D) All of the above options..

The correct answer is A.

18. **The components of highway and expressway guide signs are as follows:**

A) Black characters on an orange backdrop.

B) White letters on a green background.

C) Black letters on a yellow background.

D) White letters on a red background.

The correct answer is B.

19. What kind of road sign indicates a two-way highway?

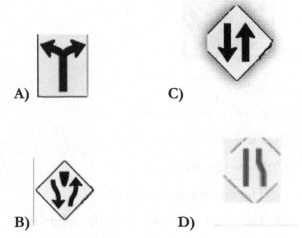

A)

B)

C)

D)

The correct answer is C

20. This sign stands for one of the following:

A) Intersection.

B) A winding road.

C) A turn to the right.

D) Switching lanes.

The correct answer is A.

21. What does this symbol mean?

A) Stop.

B) Avoid making U-turns.

C) Yield.

D) Do not proceed.

The correct answer is D.

22. This sign notifies you of the following:

DIP

A) there is a low point on the road.

B) the shoulders are soft.

C) be cautious around pedestrians.

D) you must halt immediately.

The correct answer is A.

23. At an intersection with no stop line but a stop sign and a crosswalk, you must stop:

A) prior to crossing the roadway.

B) 50 feet before the intersection.

C) before the expected placement of the stop line.

D) with your vehicle's front wheels in the crosswalk.

The correct answer is A.

24. The center lane, denoted by an arrow, is for:

A) only routine travel.

B) only making left turns.

C) passing only.

D) rescue vehicles.

The correct answer is B.

25. What does this street sign suggest?

A) Move more slowly; children are playing.

B) Keep an eye out for pedestrians crossing the street.

C) Pedestrians must remain on the sidewalk.

D) Come to a complete stop immediately ahead.

The correct answer is B.

26. What does this sign informs you of?

A) Turns are not permitted on this road.

B) The road ahead becomes narrower as you proceed.

C) The road ahead has multiple curves.

D) When it rains, the paved surface becomes slick.

The correct answer is C.

27. What does this sign imply?

A) Upcoming crossroads.

B) The current structure.

C) The road curves ahead.

D) Traffic lanes changes ahead.

The correct answer is C.

28. What does traffic sign with this shape and color represent?

A) A no-passing zone.

B) In the incorrect direction.

C) A railroad bridge.

D) Stop.

The correct answer is A.

29. What does this traffic sign represent?

A) There are pedestrians ahead.

B) The termination of a work zone.

C) The imminent school crossing.

D) There is a flag person ahead.

The correct answer is D.

30. What does the following symbol mean?

A) A piece of roadside litter.

B) Traffic should use the right side.

C) There is a sharp left turn on the road.

D) Point of convergence in front.

The correct answer is C.

31. This traffic sign directs drivers to:

A) move more slowly; children are playing.

B) keep an eye out for pedestrians crossing the street.

C) watch out for pedestrians using the sidewalk.

D) immediately come to a complete halt ahead.

The correct answer is B.

32. You must _____ when you come to a stop sign, crosswalk, but no stop line.

A) come to a halt before the crosswalk

B) come to a complete stop 50 feet before the intersection

C) come to a complete stop where you believe the stop line is

D) stop with your vehicle's front wheels in the crosswalk

The correct answer is A.

33. This symbol represents:

A) road modifications.

B) trekking trails ahead.

C) There is a hotel ahead of you.

D) a hospital.

The correct answer is D.

34. What do you make of this sign?

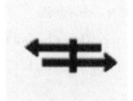

A) Make a left or right turn.

B) An impending T-intersection.

C) The route is intersected by a divided roadway.

D) An overpass is situated above a divided highway.

The correct answer is C.

35. This sign denotes:

A) All vehicles must turn right.

B) There is a side road.

C) All traffic must go in a straight line.

D) No right turns are allowed.

The correct answer is B.

36. This sign depicts one of the following:

A) Intersection.

B) A bend on the road.

C) Take the first right.

D) Lane change.

The correct answer is A.

37. How do you interpret this sign?

A) The end of a divided highway.

B) You will encounter one-way traffic ahead of you.

C) You will encounter two-way traffic ahead of you.

D) You should keep to the right.

The correct answer is D.

38. What does this sign refer to?

A) Only pedestrians may cross.

B) There is a traffic light ahead.

C) There are some trekking trails ahead.

D) There is a school crossing ahead.

The correct answer is D.

39. What does this symbol mean?

A) Make a left turn while maintaining a speed of at least 25 mph.

B) Make a right turn while maintaining a speed of at least 25 mph.

C) Take a right with a maximum safe speed of 25 mph.

D) Take a left turn with a maximum safe speed of 25 mph.

The correct answer is C.

40. What does this sign say?

A) Turn right at the next intersection.

B) The end of a split roadway.

C) The road in front of you is one-way.

D) The road ahead is closed.

The correct answer is B.

41. This symbol means:

A) there are no left turns permitted.

B) stopping is not permitted.

C) U-turns are not permitted.

D) a detour will be required.

The correct answer is C

42. What does the symbol entail?

A) There are four lanes of traffic on the road ahead.

B) There is an upcoming split highway.

C) Two-way traffic ahead.

D) There is a junction ahead.

The correct answer is C.

43. What does this sign entail?

A) Make a right turn.

B) A T-intersection.

C) A lane change.

D) A winding road.

The correct answer is B.

44. How do you interpret this sign?

A) As the path narrows, the right lane comes to an end.

B) There is a split highway ahead.

C) A hill on the left.

D) A truck is about to cross the street.

The correct answer is A.

45. This traffic sign says:

A) the divided roadway concludes.

B) a one-way street is going to commence.

C) a one-way roadway ends in front.

D) the beginning of the split roadway.

The correct answer is D.

46. What message does this symbol convey?

A) All traffic must make a left turn.

B) Do not turn left.

C) Avoid turning around.

D) A truck route is to the left.

The correct answer is B.

47. A diamond-shaped yellow and black sign, like the one shown below:

A) Notifies road users of potentially hazardous situations on or near the road.

B) Assists drivers in locating cities and towns ahead.

C) Inform drivers about traffic laws and regulations.

D) Notify drivers of ongoing road construction work.

The correct answer is A.

48. What does this symbol entail?

A) Maintain your current pace.

B) You must stop completely in front of the sign.

C) Speeding is not permitted.

D) You are approaching a traffic light.

The correct answer is D.

49. This symbol notifies you of the following:

A) It is not advisable to consume alcohol if you intend to drive.

B) The road is slick when it is wet.

C) The road ahead curves.

D) A slope is approaching.

The correct answer is B.

50. Which of these road signs represents the end of a divided highway?

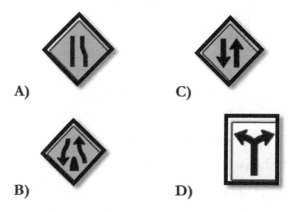

The correct answer is B

51. **Which of the following statements about vehicles flashing a diamond-shaped symbol, as pictured, is correct?**

A) They are not permitted to drive on freeways.

B) They are not permitted to exceed 35 mph.

C) They must come to a complete stop before stepping onto the tracks.

D) They are always the first to go.

The correct answer is C.

52. **What exactly does this signal mean?**

A) Only trucks weighing less than 18,000 pounds are allowed.

B) There is a hill ahead.

C) The following truck stop.

D) No trucks are permitted.

The correct answer is B.

53. If a traffic signal fails, you should:

A) stop if there are other automobiles on the road.

B) reduce your speed and, if required, come to a complete halt.

C) come to a complete halt and then resume driving when it is safe to do so.

D) continue past the intersection.

The correct answer is C.

54. What action should you take if a red flashing light appears at an intersection?

A) Pass through the intersection going straight without braking.

B) Slow down, but let oncoming traffic pass first.

C) Wait for the green light to appear before entering.

D) Hold off until it is secure before entering.

The correct answer is D.

55. The green arrow in this case denotes WHAT?

A) Feel free to utilize this lane.

B) This lane is not allowed to be used by any traffic.

C) You may make your first move.

D) You must cross over to this lane.

The correct answer is A.

56. Which of the following recommendations must a driver follow more closely than the others?

A) A constant flashing red light.

B) A police officer.

C) A stop sign.

D) A flashing red light.

The correct answer is B.

57. Which of the following statements is accurate when a driver is in a designated turn lane marked by a green arrow?

A) They must yield to pedestrians and cars in the intersection.

B) All oncoming traffic has stopped due to red lights.

C) The driver can proceed with the turn indicated without looking for approaching traffic.

D) Every choice listed previously is correct.

The correct answer is B.

58. **What should you do if you encounter an emergency vehicle behind you while driving and its lights are flashing?**

A) Pull over to the right side of the road and stop completely.

B) Quicken your speed of travel to get through traffic.

C) Slow down while staying in your lane.

D) None of the preceding.

The correct answer is A.

59. **When a red light at a railroad crossing flashes, a driver must STOP:**

A) only when a train is coming.

B) 10 feet before the signal.

C) then move forward when it is safe to do so.

D) then slow down before crossing.

The correct answer is C.

60. **When the light turns green while you are driving, there are still other motor vehicles in the intersection. How should you proceed?**

A) Hold off until every automobile and other traffic has passed through the intersection.

B) Only move forward if you can safely maneuver around the others.

C) Cross the road as you wait for the traffic to halt.

D) Sound the horn to let people know you're around.

   The correct answer is A.

61. **What should a driver do as they approach an intersection with a yellow signal light flashing?**

A) Keep driving at the same pace while keeping an eye out for others.

B) Fully halt before crossing.

C) Slow down and cross the street with utmost care.

D) Allow the light to turn green.

   The correct answer is C.

62. **When a school bus is stopped in front of you on your side of the road with flashing red lights, you must do one of the following:**

A) Stop right away.

B) Alternate lanes, move slowly, and pass cautiously.

C) Continue going until all of the children have left.

D) Go slowly and keep going unless the bus driver signals otherwise.

The correct answer is A.

63. A driver should move forward when there is a green arrow, but first:

A) they should scan the car behind them in the rearview mirror.

B) they should halt for five seconds before continuing.

C) stop for all or any oncoming vehicles and give way.

D) give way to all traffic, excluding pedestrians.

The correct answer is C.

64. It is forbidden to enter a junction:

A) if you are unable to cross without halting traffic on any side.

B) if you can't use the lane you wish to.

C) if a yellow light is indicating.

D) if you're still driving even if the light is blinking yellow.

The correct answer is A.

65. **As seen in the illustration below, a traffic signal with a green arrow and a red light means:**

A) there is just one direction you can go

B) you are only allowed to move in the direction shown by the green arrow

C) you have to be patient and watch for the green light

D) all moving vehicles, regardless of direction, must come to an immediate halt

The correct answer is B

66. **When _____, use turn signals.**

A) changing lanes and turning

B) entering and exiting freeways

C) moving closer to or further away from a roadside or curb

D) All of the aforementioned possibilities are correct

The correct answer is D.

67. **Is it a good practice for a motorist to go immediately if they are stopped at a crossroads and the traffic signal light has just turned green?**

A) The motorist currently has the right of way.

B) Yes, however the motorist must yield to any other vehicles or pedestrians in the intersection.

C) They must yield to other automobiles and pedestrians.

D) If they continues through the intersection, yes.

The correct answer is B. m

68. **The appearance of _____ is indicated by a constant yellow glow.**

A) a flashing yellow light

B) a steady supply of green light

C) continuous red lights

D) flashing red lights

The correct answer is C.

69. **If you come to a halt at a red traffic signal at a two-way street intersection, you may perform one of these:**

A) Drive immediately ahead if there are no obstructions in your path.

B) Unless otherwise depicted, turn left if the path is clear.

C) Unless otherwise depicted, turn right if the path is clear.

D) None of the above.

The correct answer is C.

Drug and alcohol test.

19 Test questions

1. **Which of the following mental illnesses does not make driving dangerous?**

A) Anger.

B) Sadness.

C) Impatience.

D) None of the above.

The correct answer is D.

2. **Because of _____ cutting a drug has the potential to be lethal.**

A) the faster rate of liver metabolism,

B) the mineral buildup that occurs in the organs as a result,

C) the resulting wide range of medicine potency,

D) B and C,

The correct answer is D.

3. **Which of the following statements about driving and drug usage is true?**

A) Only illegal drugs can damage your ability to drive.

B) Even over-the-counter drugs can affect your ability to drive.

C) You may take any prescription medication if you do not feel drowsy.

D) None of the preceding.

The correct answer is B.

4. One of the hazards of pain relievers is as follows:

A) Excessive buildup of stomach lining.

B) Liver damage and blood coagulation.

C) Damage to the liver, blood thinning, and photosensitivity.

D) None of the preceding alternatives.

The correct answer is C.

5. Which of the following is a long-term alcohol user's implication?

A) Gastritis.

B) Ulcers in the stomach.

C) Heartburn.

D) All of the above options.

The correct answer is D.

6. Which of these has effects similar to LSD but is more strongly related with tiredness, a lessened sense of self, and dulled senses?

A) Antihistamines.

B) Barbiturates.

C) Dissociative.

D) Opioids.

The correct answer is C.

7. The most prevalent cause of alcohol-related mortality is traffic accidents, followed by ___.

A) homicides and drug toxicity

B) suicides and falls

C) homicides and suicides

D) drug overdose and falls

The correct answer is C.

8. Drinking coffee after consumption of alcoholic beverages:

A) reduces blood alcohol content.

B) counteract the effects of alcohol.

C) has no effect on blood alcohol concentrations (BAC).

D) elevates blood alcohol levels.

The correct answer is C.

9. Excessive _____ use can lead to emphysema, heart disease, stroke, impotence, infertility, stress, and cancer of various organs.

A) tobacco

B) heroin

C) cocaine

D) alcohol

The correct answer is A.

10. Which of the following is the only feasible method for lowering blood alcohol level?

A) Drinking coffee.

B) By engaging in physical activity.

C) Giving your body time to detox from the alcohol.

D) Taking a short, cold shower.

The correct answer is C.

11. Which of the following is NOT a reason why young people are more prone to substance abuse?

A) Their organs are more susceptible to alcohol's effects.

B) They have greater chances to drink alcohol.

C) They have not developed more effective coping techniques.

D) They are unsure how alcohol may affect their bodies.

The correct answer is B.

12. Who is in charge of understanding how drugs affect your driving?

A) You.

B) Your physician.

C) Your local pharmacy.

D) The DMV employee.

The correct answer is A.

13. What effect could the combination of alcohol and another substance have on your blood?

A) It will enhance the effects of both.

B) It will not impede your ability to drive.

C) It decreases the effects of the drug or therapy.

D) It will mitigate the effects of alcohol.

The correct answer is A.

14. How much alcohol can you consume and still drive safely?

A) None.

B) Half a drink.

C) One alcoholic drink.

D) Two alcoholic drinks.

The correct answer is A.

15. Other than alcohol, what drugs can impair one's driving ability?

A) Antihistamines.

B) Marijuana.

C) A cooling treatment.

D) All of the above options.

The correct answer is D.

16. What are the resultant effects of driving under the influence of alcohol or other drugs?

A) Imprisonment is the most likely outcome.

B) Loss of a driver's license.

C) All of the above options

D) A monetary fine.

The correct answer is D.

17. How long does it take the human body on average to digest the alcohol in 12 ounces of beer?

A) One hour.

B) A day.

C) Five minutes.

D) It takes 5 hours.

The correct answer is A.

18. What becomes of your driver's license if you refuse to take a breath or blood test?

A) No evidence exists to convict you of drunk driving.

B) You cannot be arrested for driving under the influence.

C) Your driver's license will be revoked.

D) None of the above.

The correct answer is C.

19. Marijuana consumption has the following short-term effects:

A) A lack of coordination.

B) Dizziness.

C) A rise in heart rate.

D) All of the preceding options.

The correct answer is D.

License renewal test.

20 Test questions

1. **Before changing lanes, check the lane next to you by:**

A) looking over your right shoulder.

B) examining your rearview mirror.

C) reversing your direction and gazing down the lane you're about to enter.

D) casting a glance over your left shoulder.

   The correct answer is C.

2. **Do not drive across a solid double yellow line in the middle of the road:**

A) to take a left.

B) to enter a private driveway.

C) to avoid colliding with other vehicles.

D) None of the preceding.

   The correct answer is C.

3. **If you're in the left lane of a four-lane freeway and want to exit on the right, you must _____.**

A) carefully cross all four lanes at once

B) increase your speed to the point where you outpace all other traffic on the highway

C) take your time when changing lanes

D) To get into the right lane, switch lanes one at a time

The correct answer is D.

4. Which of these should be obeyed above the others?

A) A steady red light.

B) A member of the police force.

C) A stop sign.

D) A flashing red light.

The correct answer is B.

5. Crossers at corners have the right of way:

A) only at designated intersections.

B) st all crosswalks, marked or unmarked.

C) unless there is a crosswalk on the street.

D) only when passing through a green signal.

The correct answer is B.

6. If you are driving while under the influence of a non-prescription substance, you should:

A) read the labels before getting behind the wheel.

B) instead, drink booze.

C) get in the driver's seat.

D) only drive during daytime hours.

The correct answer is A.

7. Which of the following statements about road workers is false?

A) The color of road equipment is orange.

B) Fines for certain violations in construction zones are increased.

C) White signs indicate impending lane restrictions.

D) All of the preceding options.

The correct answer is C.

8. Observing warning hazard lights on a moving passenger vehicle implies:

A) circumnavigate in the opposite direction.

B) come to a halt by tugging on the right shoulder.

C) a hazard or an accident is possible.

D) the passenger vehicle takes precedence.

The correct answer is C.

9. When making a right turn on a green signal, you must _____.

A) continue driving at your normal speed

B) come to a complete stop and check for traffic

C) make way for pedestrians

D) accelerate

The correct answer is C.

10. A "no stopping" sign indicates that, unless otherwise instructed by a police officer or traffic officer, you may only stop _____.

A) to unload packages

B) to prevent collisions with other vehicles

C) to register visitors

D) for a maximum of five minutes

   The correct answer is B.

11. How do you start a U-turn on a divided street with numerous lanes in your direction?

A) Take the left lane.

B) Move to the left lane.

C) In the center lane.

D) Any of the prior options.

   The correct answer is B.

12. If a green arrow turns into a green light, as shown below, you:

A) may continue to turn, but you must yield to oncoming traffic.

B) No longer able to turn and must continue straight.

C) You still have the right of way.

D) You are no longer required to turn in the arrow's direction.

The correct answer is A.

13. If a car approaches you at night and does not turn off its high beams, look:

A) toward the center of the road.

B) on the right-hand-section of the road.

C) on the left -hand-part of the road.

D) keep straight forward in your lane.

The correct answer is B.

14. When passing on a two-lane road, you should consider:

A) your speed in relation to others and your ability to accelerate.

B) the quantity of clear space you must traverse.

C) the speed and distance of approaching vehicles, as well as any potential hazards.

D) None of the preceding.

The correct answer is D.

15. **Which of the following assertions concerning slick roads is correct?**

A) In shady places, hidden ice spots may freeze first and dry last.

B) Bridges and overpasses are the first to freeze, followed by highways.

C) Wet leaves induce sliding, and moist ice is slicker than ice alone.

D) None of the preceding.

The correct answer is D.

16. **This is what this road sign says:**

A) There are no turns allowed on this road.

B) The road narrows as you travel forward.

C) As you proceed, you will meet a series of curves.

D) If it rains, the road may get slick.

The correct answer is C.

17. How do you interpret this road sign?

A) The divided highway comes to an end.

B) The one-way street begins.

C) The one-way street reaches its end.

D) The split roadway begins.

The correct answer is D.

18. This sign is meant to inform motorists of the following:

A) An upcoming crossroads.

B) A current road-building project.

C) Curves on the road ahead.

D) Changes in road lane.

The correct answer is C.

19. It is prohibited to enter a junction if:

A) you cannot cross without stopping traffic on either side.

B) there is a traffic jam in the lane you want to utilize.

C) the light has a yellow tinge to it.

D) you did not stop before the yellow light began to blink.

The correct answer is A.

20. If there are still motor vehicles in the intersection when your red light turns green, you must _____.

A) cross the road and wait for the traffic to clear

B) proceed only if you can safely maneuver around the other vehicles

C) stop and wait for traffic to clear the intersection before continuing

D) Since you have the right of way, proceed through the intersection.

The correct answer is C.

Adult permit test

30 Test questions

1. **It is acceptable to park in front of a driveway:**

A) never under any circumstances.

B) as long as it's only parked for 15 minutes.

C) if your house is directly across from the driveway.

D) if a friend owns the driveway.

The correct answer is A.

2. **If there are two double solid yellow lines in the middle of the roadway, you may:**

A) cross them to make a left turn into a private driveway.

B) cross them to make a right turn into a private driveway.

C) must be viewed as a solid barrier that must never be breached.

D) you may cross it to avoid slower-moving vehicles.

The correct answer is A.

3. **_____ mark the opposing traffic lanes.**

A) White lines

B) Lines in red

C) Striking lines

D) Lines in orange

The correct answer is D.

4. When changing lanes on a multi-lane roadway, you should:

A) horn.

B) switch on your headlights.

C) reduce your speed.

D) check your mirrors and blind areas.

The correct answer is A.

5. If you wish to change lanes, you should:

A) check over the right shoulder to make sure the lane next to you is clear.

B) examine your rearview mirror.

C) examine the environment around the lane you're about to enter.

D) look over your left shoulder.

The correct answer is C.

6. When approaching an intersection, you must yield to:

A) the vehicle in the intersection.

B) the vehicle on your right.

C) the opposing traffic lane car.

D) the car to your left.

The correct answer is A.

7. Which of the following assertions about other drivers is true?

A) They always obey traffic signals and signs.

B) Those who use turn signals always make the correct turn.

C) Never assume that you always have the right of way.

D) Drivers of larger vehicles are safer.

The correct answer is C.

8. What should you do if you are following too closely and another car cuts you off?

A) Enter the next lane.

B) Apply the brakes firmly.

C) Drive to the side of the road and come to a complete halt.

D) Remove your foot off the gas.

The correct answer is D.

9. Which of the following assertions about cars with diamond-shaped signs is correct?

A) They are not permitted to go on highways.

B) They are not allowed to exceed 35 miles per hour.

C) They must come to a complete stop before crossing railroad tracks.

D) They have the right of way at all times.

The correct answer is C.

10. If the weather is extremely foggy, slow down and turn on the _____.

A) lights with a low beam

B) lights with a high intensity

C) emergency lights that flash

D) wiper blades on the windscreen

The correct answer is A.

11. A steady yellow light at a crossing indicates:

A) Go.

B) Allow other vehicles to pass.

C) Slow down and prepare to come to a complete halt.

D) Stop.

Answer: C.

12. What colors are the warning signs that highlight hazards ahead, such as road curves or narrow bridges?

A) A white backdrop with black text or symbols on it.

B) Yellow with black writing or symbols on a yellow background.

C) Blue with white lettering or symbols on a blue background.

D) Green with white writing or symbols on a green background.

The correct answer is B.

13. What colors are used to indicate the distance to the next highway exit on a sign?

A) Yellow with black writing on a yellow background.

B) White letters on a black backdrop.

C) A red background with white letters.

D) A green background with white letters.

The correct answer is D.

14. If a truck behind you intends to pass you, your speed should:

A) remain steady or decrease.

B) change the speed.

C) pick up the pace.

D) change lanes.

The correct answer is A.

15. Why should drivers and passengers adjust the headrests of their vehicle seats?

A) It helps to relax and relieve the stress of driving.

B) To help prevent and treat neck injuries.

C) It helps residents maintain their haircuts.

D) To stay focused if they are tired.

The correct answer is B.

16. Which of the following is a defensive driving rule?

A) Keep a straight face.

B) Remain alert and keep your eyes roving.

C) Expect others to compensate for your mistakes.

D) Have faith in your ability to avoid danger at the last moment.

The correct answer is B.

17. **What should you do if your car begins to slip on wet pavement?**

A) Remove your foot from the gas pedal gradually.

B) Change down to a lower gear to slow down.

C) Apply the brakes quickly and forcefully to slow down.

D) Select neutral to slow down.

The correct answer is A.

18. **When departing a motorway with a downhill-curving ramp, you must:**

A) slow down to the posted freeway speed limit

B) drive around the bend without braking.

C) reduce speed to a safe level before the curve.

D) accelerate before the turn to avoid over-steering.

The correct answer is C.

19. **Where should a vehicle a driver begin their U-turn on a two-lane street with two lanes in each direction?**

A) The middle left-hand turn lane.

B) The left lane.

C) The proper lane.

D) Any available lane.

The correct answer is B.

20. As a car driver, you may drive in a bike lane:

A) during rush hour if there are no bicycles available.

B) not more than 200 feet before turning right.

C) when no bicycles are available.

D) at no point in time.

The correct answer is D.

21. What is the leading cause of rear-end collisions?

A) Constantly checking the rearview mirror.

B) Driving too close to other vehicles (Tailgating).

C) Not paying attention to details.

D) Getting around traffic.

The correct answer is B.

22. When you _____, you should widen the spacing between yourself and the car ahead of you.

A) trail a tiny passenger car

B) are encroached upon by a tailgater

C) travel at a slower speed than the posted limit

D) None of the preceding.

The correct answer is B.

23. You are stopped at a red light. Although the traffic light turns green, motor vehicles remain in the intersection. What are your alternatives?

A) Wait for the motor vehicles to clear the crossing before proceeding.

B) Proceed only if you can maneuver safely around the other vehicles.

C) Continue through the intersection while traffic clears.

D) Sound the horn to alert others to your presence, then go through the intersection.

The correct answer is A.

24. This sign stands for:

A) Maintain your current speed.

B) You must come to an abrupt halt.

C) Speeding is strictly prohibited.

D) A traffic signal is ahead.

The correct answer is D.

25. What should you be concerned about if you encounter this sign?

A) Driving with misaligned headlights because one side of the car is higher than the other.

B) Tire damage if you slide onto the shoulder.

C) Hydroplaning if the shoulder is wet.

D) Vehicle control loss if you slide onto the shoulder as a result of a drop-off.

The correct answer is D.

26. When passing other automobiles, you should:

A) assume they will keep a constant speed.

B) assume that if you use your turn signal, they will let you pass.

C) not expect them to let you return to your lane.

D) assume that if you try to pass, they will apply the brakes.

The correct answer is C.

27. Who is accountable for understanding how your drugs affect your ability to drive?

A) You.

B) Your doctor.

C) Your local pharmacy.

D) The DMV employee.

The correct answer is A.

28. **When passing another vehicle, you should do the following:**

A) Flash your headlights to alert them.

B) Use your four-way flashers to alert others.

C) Properly signal your intention to change lanes.

D) Use your horn to draw the driver's attention.

The correct answer is C.

29. **Which of the following is an example of a safe driving technique?**

A) Inspecting your rearview mirrors on a regular basis.

B) Maintaining a view of the road ahead.

C) In the fog, turn on your high-beam lights.

D) Tailgating.

The correct answer is A.

30. **What effect does drinking have on your driving ability and judgment?**

A) It boosts your driving abilities while impairing your judgment.

B) It impairs driving ability as well as judgment.

C) It has no effect on driving skills or judgment.

D) It has no effect on judgment but is harmful to driving abilities.

The correct answer is B.

Tips for Passing Your Driving Test

Here are some pointers for passing the South Carolina road test and becoming a licensed driver, whether you are getting your license for the first time or a senior with a lapsed renewal:

- ✓ Extend courtesy to the examiner by greeting and be polite throughout the exam period.
- ✓ Do not make small talk; respond to questions and directions.
- ✓ Be attentive.
- ✓ Brake very smoothly and gently.
- ✓ Employ the use of your turn signal for every turn and lane change.
- ✓ Use head movements when checking mirrors, looking to turn, or checking the right-of- way.
- ✓ It may be of help to put on a hat to draw attention to these movements.
- ✓ Never cross the lines at intersections or crossroads.
- ✓ Give a listening ear to everything the instructor says.
- ✓ Do not do anything that is not asked for.
- ✓ Do not exceed the posted/approved speed limit.
- ✓ Try to drive the route or become familiar with the area.

- ✓ Arrive early and take a tour of the neighborhood.

- ✓ Allow three to four car lengths between you and the motorist directly in front of you.

- ✓ When you change lanes or make a turn, turn your head to look behind you rather than relying on mirrors.

- ✓ Steer smoothly and with the right hand in the proper position.

- ✓ Keep to the right-hand portion of the lane.

- ✓ Keep your attention on the road and never try to read what the examiner is writing on their page.

- ✓ Avoid reducing speed when switching lanes; instead, follow the direction of the traffic.

- ✓ Be sure to get in the car with the radio switched off.

- ✓ At the end of the test, thank the examiner.

What Examiners Normally Look Forward To

Approaching a crossing:

✓   Enter the appropriate area and scan both directions.

Observe right-of-way:

✓ Stop and yield to emergency vehicles, pull over for pedestrians, and do not enter intersections where you will restrict other traffic.

Directly into parking:

✓ Move directly into the available parking space. When parked appropriately, the car should be positioned in the spot and should not extend into the traffic lane under any circumstances.

✓ If there is no vertical curve (elevation) on your driving test, the STOP/START ON GRADE maneuver is mimicked by parking in a straight line or pulling over to the side of the road prior to the turnabout maneuver.

✓   You will be requested to demonstrate or explain to the examiner what you would do if you had to keep the car parked on an elevation or a flat area, with or without a curb.

✓ Stop quickly. Travel at 20 mph and come to a swift, safe stop when asked to do so by the examiner.

Backing up:

✓ Slowly and gently back for a distance of about 50 feet. When backing up, do not employ the use of the rear-view mirror. The best option is to look behind you by turning your head.

Conform to stop sign:

✓ If making s turn, give the proper signal, approach in the appropriate lane, stop completely before reaching the pedestrian crosswalk or stop line, and remain stopped until you can safely drive without inhibiting with cross traffic.

Traffic signals must be obeyed:

✓ Drive into the appropriate lane and towards the light at a pace that allows you to stop if the light alternates.

✓ Stop before the pedestrian crosswalk or stop line if required.

✓ When the signal shows green, wait until all other vehicles and pedestrians are clear of the intersection before continuing.

✓ Indicate with the appropriate stop and turn signals.

✓ Do well to observe "no turn" and "one way" signs.

Give signal and turn:

✓ Proceed into the appropriate lane and indicate your turn for the last 100 feet.

✓ Prior to reaching the crosswalk, slow down your speed and merge into the proper lane.

Passing:

✓ Always glance in front and behind you to pass safely.

✓ Unless the automobile ahead is preparing to make a left turn or is in the left turn lane on a roadway with more than one lane in each direction, pass on the left-hand-side.

✓ It is illegal to pass on the shoulder (side of the road).

Keep to the appropriate lane:

✓ Except on one-way streets, drive in the right lane.

✓ Change lanes only when it is not hazardous.

Trail at a SAFE distance.

✓ Under no circumstance should you follow other vehicles too closely.

Driving posture:

✓ Maintain correct posture by keeping both hands firmly on the steering wheel and not resting your elbow **on the car's side window.**

Frequently asked questions

What Questions are on the Permit Test?
- The written knowledge test covers the contents of the North Carolina Driver's Manual, such as road signs, road rules and safe driving practices. There 30 multiple choice questions, and you must answer at least 24 correctly to pass.

What am I required to carry out in My Driving Test in NC?
During the road/driving test, you will:

- Switch on your headlights and windshield wipers.
- Switch on your turn signals: inclusive of the four-way hazard lights
- Test your brake lights.
- Make lane changes.
- Make right and left turns.
- Identify road signs.
- Parallel park.
- Perform a 100 feet backing.

What is the Cost of the North Carolina Permit Test?

o It is $2.00 for a knowledge test and $2.50 for the beginner's.

How Long Does the Road Test Take?

o One hour is the maximum time allowed for the road test. You will be required to successfully perform the following actions:

1. Switch on your headlights and windshield wipers.

What are the Requirements for Obtaining f Driver's Permit in North Carolina?

o To obtain a driver's permit you must first apply for a beginner's permit and pass the vision and knowledge tests.

o You must provide your social security number.

o You must bring required documents such as a government-issued birth certificate, and proof of your current physical address of residence.

How Long Do I Have To Wait To Retake Permit Test In North Carolina?

o As a rookie driver, you must wait at least 2 weeks. After the second attempt you must wait 60 days before another re-sit.

Is It Necessary to Retest if I Intend to Renew My North Carolina Permit?

- o   If your beginner's permit is expired by at least nine months, you must visit a North Carolina DMV office nearest to you for renewal, otherwise you must take the knowledge test again.

Am I Required to Retake Driving Test When Moving to NC?

- o   Yes, to obtain your NC driver's license, you will have to retake and pass the written exam.

What are the Different Types of Driver's License in North Carolina?

- o   Regular class (Class D).
- o   Commercial driver's license (Classes A, B, C).
- o   Class D: with this you can move from one place to another.

Is it Possible to get My Driver's License without Taking a Road Test?

- o   No, except for a moped license, you must take and pass a vision, knowledge, and road tests.

What is the Required Age to Apply for a Permit in NC?

- o   18 years of age is the acceptable age to apply.

- o   15 years of age for a regular or motorcycle beginner's permit. If you are under 18, you must bring a person listed on the Consent for Minor (SCDMV Form 447-CM) with you to consent.

What is the Cost of License Renewal in North Carolina?

- o $25.
- o   Provide the name of your vehicle insurance company.

Made in the USA
Columbia, SC
02 September 2024

41488595R00068